GRAPHIC BIOGRAPHIES

FLORENCE NIGHTINGALE
Lady with the Lamp

by Trina Robbins

illustrated by Anne Timmons

Consultant:
Laurie K. Glass, RN, PhD, FAAN
Professor Emerita
University of Wisconsin-Milwaukee

Capstone

Graphic Library is published by Capstone Press.
151 Good Counsel Drive, P.O. Box 669, Mankato, Minnesota 56002.
www.capstonepress.com

1 2 3 4 5 6 12 11 10 09 08 07

Library of Congress Cataloging-in-Publication Data
Robbins, Trina.
    Florence Nightingale: lady with the lamp / by Trina Robbins; illustrated by Anne Timmons.
    p. cm. —(Graphic library. Graphic biographies)
    Summary: "In graphic novel format, tells the life story of Florence Nightingale, the English nurse
who reformed military hospitals during the Crimean War and became the founder of modern nursing"—
Provided by publisher.
    Includes bibliographical references and index.
    ISBN-13: 978-0-7368-6850-1 (hardcover)
    ISBN-10: 0-7368-6850-X (hardcover)
    ISBN-13: 978-0-7368-7902-6 (softcover pbk.)
    ISBN-10: 0-7368-7902-1 (softcover pbk.)
    1. Nightingale, Florence, 1820–1910—Juvenile literature. 2. Nurses—England—Biography—
Juvenile literature. I. Timmons, Anne, ill. II. Title. III. Series.
RT37.N5R63 2007
610.73092—dc22
[B]
                                                                                          2006025905

Designer
Alison Thiele

Production Designers
Renée Doyle and Kim Brown

Colorist
Brent Schoonover

Editor
Christine Peterson

Editor's note: Direct quotations from primary sources are indicated by a yellow background.

Direct quotations appear on the following pages:
Page 6, from an 1849 diary entry by Florence Nightingale as published in *Florence
    Nightingale: Mystic, Visionary, Healer* by Barbara Montgomery Dossey (Springhouse,
    Pa.: Springhouse Corporation, 2000).
Page 10, from an 1851 letter by Florence Nightingale, as published in *The Collected Works
    of Florence Nightingale*, edited by Lynn McDonald (Waterloo, Ontario, Canada:
    Wilfrid Laurier University Press, 2004).

TABLE OF CONTENTS

Chapter 1
A Life of Luxury

Florence Nightingale was born to a wealthy English family. Unlike most people in the 1800s, her father believed girls should be educated. William Nightingale taught French, history, and mathematics to young Florence and her sister, Parthenope.

The pen of my aunt is on the table.

La plume de ma tante est sur la table.

Your French is improving, Florence.

Parthenope, pay attention. You need to learn this.

Why, Father? I'll have no use for French. I just want to find a good husband to marry.

By the time Florence was 19, she was often asked to nurse sick relatives and neighbors. Florence did not have any training. She simply did what she thought was right.

This tea should help you feel better.

Florence, you are an angel. I couldn't stand to have a hired nurse from the city care for me.

Throughout the 1800s, most nurses were not well respected. Many nurses were unclean and uneducated.

While traveling in Europe, Florence visited Kaiserwerth, Germany. Florence soon decided what she wanted to do with her life.

I want to become a nurse, but I have much to learn.

Respectable women can study nursing at our school in Kaiserwerth.

Chapter 2
A Call to Nursing

Florence's mother and sister were horrified by her decision to become a nurse.

Mother, we'll be disgraced. Forbid Florence from becoming a nurse.

Florence, nurses are poor and not respected. You are a refined lady. How can you be a nurse?

Mother, I know what my calling is in life. I want to be a nurse and care for the sick and less fortunate.

Against her family's wishes, Florence went to Germany in 1851 to study nursing at the Institution of Deaconesses at Kaiserwerth.

Because the hospital needed Florence and her nursing skills, board members decided to treat all women in need.

13

In 1854, hundreds of English soldiers were wounded in the Crimean War in Turkey. Many men suffered from diseases. These men were sent to a military hospital in Scutari, near Constantinople.

Hospital conditions were terrible. Patients had no beds or food. Doctors did not have bandages or operating tables. News of these awful conditions reached England.

TERRIBLE CONDITIONS IN MILITARY HOSPITAL

Our men are dying from the filthy conditions in these hospitals.

My son is over there fighting for the Queen. Is this how he is rewarded?

This is no way to treat our brave soldiers!

You have been called to the honorable job of nursing. Your main concern will be caring for the sick and wounded men.

You will behave in a proper manner. I will not stand for any alcohol use or rough language.

Just six days after receiving Herbert's letter, Florence had assembled a group of 38 nurses. On October 21, 1854, the women set sail for Turkey.

The women were not prepared for what they found at the hospital.

Miss Nightingale, there is no water. What shall we do?

These men are covered with lice!

Water . . . water.

UHHNNNNN

17

25

How can that be?

Filthy conditions, sir. If the hospital had a sanitation plan, we could have done more to stop diseases from spreading.

On June 24, 1860, Florence opened the Nightingale Training School for Nurses at St. Thomas' Hospital in London. When Nightingale students graduated, they became certified nurses. Nightingale nurses worked at hospitals across England.

Florence Nightingale is called the founder of modern nursing. Through her work in the Crimean War and her school, Florence helped make nursing the respected profession that it is today.

MORE ABOUT FLORENCE NIGHTINGALE

Florence Nightingale was born May 12, 1820, in Florence, Italy. Her parents named her after the city where she was born. On August 13, 1910, Florence died at age 90 in London, England.

Florence became one of the most famous women in Europe. Poems, books, and songs were written about her. Florence also had a street, racehorse, and lifeboat named in her honor.

Historians believe that the "Crimean fever" that Florence came down with might have been typhus or brucellosis. Both illnesses cause high fever.

Florence received many medals for her outstanding work. In 1883, Queen Victoria awarded her the Royal Red Cross. In 1907, King Edward VII gave Florence the Order of Merit. Florence was the first woman to receive that medal.

Florence published many books and pamphlets on hospitals, nursing, and the importance of sanitation. Her book *Notes on Nursing* sold 15,000 copies in one month and is still in print today.

Florence was the first woman elected as an honorary member of the American Statistical Association. Her ability to use statistics to show the effect of unsanitary hospital conditions earned her this honor.

 In 1861, Florence helped the U.S. government set up military hospitals during the Civil War (1861–1865).

 When Florence died, England's King Edward VII offered to have her buried in Westminster Abbey, where England's kings and heroes are buried. Instead, Florence was buried at St. Margaret's Church, in East Wellow, Hampshire. Florence had wanted a small funeral, but the churchyard at St. Margaret's was packed with people, many of them old soldiers in their uniforms.

 As a tribute to Florence, Lystra E. Gretter of the Farrand Training School for Nurses in Detroit, Michigan, wrote the Florence Nightingale Pledge in 1893. This pledge is still said at graduation ceremonies and other events honoring nurses.

GLOSSARY

cholera (KOL-ur-uh)—a disease that causes sickness and diarrhea

disgrace (diss-GRAYSS)—a reaction of shame or disapproval from others

heroine (HER-oh-uhn)—a girl or woman who shows strength and courage by doing a good thing

reputation (rep-yuh-TAY-shuhn)—your worth or character, as judged by other people

resign (ri-ZINE)—to give up a job or position voluntarily

respectable (ri-SPEK-tuh-buhl)—to behave in an honest and decent manner

sanitation (san-uh-TAY-shuhn)—to protect people from dirt and disease

INTERNET SITES

FactHound offers a safe, fun way to find Internet sites related to this book. All of the sites on FactHound have been researched by our staff.

Here's how:
1. Visit *www.facthound.com*
2. Choose your grade level.
3. Type in this book ID **073686850X** for age-appropriate sites. You may also browse subjects by clicking on letters, or by clicking on pictures and words.
4. Click on the **Fetch It** button.

FactHound will fetch the best sites for you!

READ MORE

Barnham, Kay. *Florence Nightingale: The Lady of the Lamp.* Austin, Texas: Raintree Steck-Vaughn, 2002.

Davis, Marc. *Florence Nightingale: Founder of the Nightingale School of Nursing.* Our People. Chanhassen, Minn.: Child's World, 2004.

Hinman, Bonnie. *Florence Nightingale and the Advancement of Nursing.* Uncharted, Unexplored, and Unexplained. Hockessin, Del.: Mitchell Lane, 2005.

Lynch, Emma. *Florence Nightingale.* Lives and Times. Chicago: Heinemann, 2005.

BIBLIOGRAPHY

Dossey, Barbara Montgomery. *Florence Nightingale: Mystic, Visionary, Healer.* Springhouse, Pa.: Springhouse Corporation, 2000.

Nightingale, Florence. *I Have Done My Duty: Florence Nightingale in the Crimean War, 1854–1856.* Iowa City, Iowa: University of Iowa Press, 1987.

Nightingale, Florence. *Notes on Nursing: What It Is and What It Is Not.* Philadelphia: University of Pennsylvania Printing Office, 1965.

INDEX